THE SECRET

Zoë Brigley

THE SECRET

BLOODAXE BOOKS

ISBN: 978 1 85224 787 4

First published 2007 by
Bloodaxe Books Ltd,
Highgreen,
Tarset,
Northumberland NE48 1RP.

www.bloodaxebooks.com
For further information about Bloodaxe titles
please visit our website or write to
the above address for a catalogue.

Bloodaxe Books Ltd acknowledges
the financial assistance of
Arts Council England, North East.

Cover design: Neil Astley & Pamela Robertson-Pearce.

Cover printing: J. Thomson Colour Printers Ltd, Glasgow.

Printed in Great Britain by
Bell & Bain Limited, Glasgow, Scotland.

Ac yna goddiweddodd Gwydion hithau ac y dywedodd wrthi, 'Ni'th laddaf di. Fe wnaf iti rywbeth sy'n waeth. Dyna yw hynny,' meddaf ef, 'dy ollwng di yn rhith aderyn. Ac oherwydd y cywilwydd a wnaethost ti i Leu Llaw Gyffes, na feiddia dithau dangos dy wyneb fyth liw dydd.'

Y MABINOGION

Gwydion overtook her and said, 'I will not kill you, but I will do what is worse: I will let you go in the form of a bird. Because of the shame you have brought Lleu Skilful Hand, you are never to show your face to the light of day.'

THE MABINOGION

ACKNOWLEDGEMENTS

Thanks to the Society of Authors for an Eric Gregory Award in 2003. Thanks to Academi for a miscellaneous bursary in 2005 that enabled me to visit the Na Bolom library in Mexico and to experience the Mexican Independence Day celebrations.

Thanks to those who have published my poems: Robert Minhinnick at *Poetry Wales*, Francesca Rhydderch at *The New Welsh Review*, Patricia McCarthy at *Agenda*, Rupert Loydell at *Stride Magazine*, Debbie Taylor at *Mslexia*, Amy Wack at Seren, Margaret Jacobs at *Frontiers: A Journal of Women's Studies*, Carol Baldock at *Orbis*, Jan Fortune-Wood at Cinnamon Press, Jonathan Morley at the Heaventree Press, Edward Barker at *Limelight*, Peter Thomas at *Scintilla*, Michael Hulse at *Leviathan Quarterly*, and Esther Morgan at *Reactions*.

Thanks to those who have encouraged me: David Morley, Peter Blegvad, Maureen Freely, David Hart, Gillian Clarke, Julie Boden, Pascale Petit, Deryn Rees-Jones, Menna Elfyn, Emma Mason, Helen Dennis, Gwyneth Lewis and Eva Salzman. Thanks to my friends in Wales, Mexico and elsewhere. Thank to my family, especially my mother, Jude Brigley, who introduced me to a love of language. Thanks most of all to Dan Thompson for pulling me back to earth.

CONTENTS

PREFACE   *9*

THE LESSER SECRETS

   0. Your Own Pleasure   *13*
   I. Jackdaw   *15*
  II. Our Lady of the Rock   *16*
 III. Blodeuwedd   *18*
 IV. Bedlam Bazaar   *19*
  V. The Clarinet Player   *20*
 VI. The Jewel-box   *21*
 VII. Our Lady of Situations   *22*
VIII. Our Lady of Snows   *23*
 IX. Hecate   *24*
  X. My Grandfather   *25*
 XI. Love Song For His Mother   *26*
 XII. Canopy   *27*
XIII. A Small Unit of Time   *28*
XIV. Lonesome City Dweller   *29*
 XV. The Secret   *30*
XVI. The Citadel   *31*
XVII. Epithalamion   *32*
XVIII. The Orphic Principle   *33*
 XIX. She   *35*
 XX. Metropolis   *36*
 XXI. Trade   *38*

THE GREATER SECRETS

DAY 1: From Central America   *41*
DAY 2: Ten Fingers, Ten Thumbs   *42*
DAY 3: Calendar   *43*
DAY 4: Lizard   *44*
DAY 5: Serpent   *45*
DAY 6: The Flying Bed   *46*
DAY 7: Meon Hill   *47*
DAY 8: Quarry   *48*
DAY 9: Fish-eye   *49*
DAY 10: Anaglypta   *50*
DAY 11: My Dress Hangs Here   *51*
DAY 12: My Nunning Skull   *52*
DAY 13: Everything Under the Earth   *53*
DAY 14: Saboteur   *54*
DAY 15: Yield   *55*

DAY 16: The Long-tailed Bird *56*
DAY 17: Collision *58*
DAY 18: Assassin *59*
DAY 19: The Guitar *60*
DAY 20: Journeying *61*

THE CURSE OF THE LONG-TAILED BIRD *63*

TRANSLATIONS AND GLOSSARY *88*

PREFACE

This collection emerges from silence and the secrets. It is also a journey in marginal poetry. Some of these poems mirror the needs of my own culture, my own country, Wales, but as Julia Kristeva suggests in *Strangers to Ourselves*, 'How can one avoid sinking into the mire of common sense, if not by becoming a stranger to one's own country, language, sex, and identity?' In Italo Calvino's *Invisible Cities*, the people of Baucis will not allow any part of the city to touch the earth's surface and Calvino describes the residents who 'with their spyglasses and telescopes aimed downward...never tire of examining it, tirelessly observing it, leaf by leaf, stone by stone, ant by ant'.

The book is split into three sections. The first, *The Lesser Secrets*, takes its name from one section of the Tarot pack and tries to reconcile Tarot symbols, such as the Fool, the Magician or the Emperor, to modern life. *The Greater Secrets* moves beyond Western culture using the structure of a twenty day cycle in the Aztec calendar. Each day is characterised by a symbol, such as the lizard, the snake or the eagle.

The final sequence, *The Curse of the Long-tailed Bird*, explores Mexican mythologies and Western fairytales. The verse play recycles the story of Bluebeard, but it replaces the character of Bluebeard with Hernán Cortés, the Spanish adventurer who conquered Central America, and it replaces the heroine Judith with Dona Marina, Cortés' woman from an indigenous tribe who was also known as La Malinche. There are further notes on this sequence at the back of the book, along with translations from *Cymraeg* (the Welsh language) and a glossary.

THE LESSER SECRETS
A 21 CARD TRICK

Here, said she,
Is your card, the drowned Phoenician Sailor,
(Those are pearls that were his eyes. Look!)
Here is Belladonna, the Lady of the Rocks,
the lady of situations.

T.S. ELIOT

THE LESSER SECRETS: CODEX

0.	The Fool	*Your Own Pleasure*
I.	The Magician	*Jackdaw*
II.	The Priestess	*Our Lady of the Rock*
III.	The Empress	*Blodeuwedd*
IV.	The Emperor	*Bedlam Bazaar*
V.	The Hierophant	*The Clarinet Player*
VI.	The Lovers	*The Jewel-Box*
VII.	The Chariot	*Our Lady of Situations*
VIII.	Strength	*Our Lady of Snows*
IX.	The Hermit	*Hecate*
X.	The Wheel	*My Grandfather*
XI.	The Scales	*Love Song For His Mother*
XII.	The Hanged Man	*Canopy*
XIII.	Death	*A Small Unit of Time*
XIV.	Temperance	*Lonesome City Dweller*
XV.	The Devil	*The Secret*
XVI.	The Tower	*The Citadel*
XVII.	The Star	*Infinity*
XVIII.	The Moon	*The Orphic Principle*
XIX.	The Sun	*She*
XX.	Judgement	*Metropolis*
XXI.	The World	*Trade*

0. My Own Pleasure

*A pleasure whose origin is to be placed outside us and in
objects whose presence we cannot be sure of; a pleasure
therefore that is precarious in itself, undermined by the
fear of loss.*

MICHEL FOUCAULT

I search for you in the city:
I search for you in the city,
scan each face I pass, note each tree.
Scan each face I pass, note each tree.
I scan for you in the pass, note each city;
I search each face in the tree.

The bright shop window you'll see;
the bright shop window you'll see
with her: it's strange that you're so close
with her. It's strange that you're so close.
The bright, her window; strange that you'll close
with its shop – see that you're so.

When it grows dark the streets;
when it grows dark; the streets
are a mass of bodies, lights and cars,
are a mass of bodies, lights and cars.
When the bodies a-mass, dark cars
are it: the streets of grows and lights.

You exist somewhere   without;
you exist somewhere   without
me in the heaving mess:
me in the heaving mess.
Me somewhere. Exist heaving.
You in the mess   without.

I stop to buy a newspaper;
I stop to buy a newspaper.
Long columns of words remind me;
long columns of words remind me.
Me? I long to column a newspaper,
stop to remind: buy of words.

Long, striped fields outside Vienna.
Long striped fields outside Vienna
seen when I flew home early.
Seen when I flew home early.
Long seen fields when Vienna flew;
I striped home (outside early).

You were to follow, but then –
You were to follow, but then
like now, something snapped inside me.
Like now, something snapped inside me.
You follow now to inside, like me,
but then you were something snapped.

I foresee you alone:
I foresaw you. Strange that you'll close
seeing field, word, light;
heaving field, word, light.
Long seen words snap alone:
I am fields you light.

I. Jackdaw

*False are the ways of a woman, in words and deeds alike,
and although she may seem fair to behold, it is the result
of laborious use of pigments, and if she is stripped of these
many devices, she is like the jackdaw that was plucked of
its feathers in the fable.*

ACHILLES TATIUS

Each night, she would sleep in his bed,
and morning would break early: she locked herself in the day,

no bathroom, only windows: a mirror, tubes, tweezers, bottles,
the finger split gape and translucent sweets.

Rose lips of milk wash paint her a new skin;
(Elizabeth) filling gouges, a weeping face with sores.

Thick-black lead whispers from lashes:
a jar of pupils and shelled eye-lids

For the wafer, rose lips rub away the gloss
– a patch of flash – between tongue and teeth:

Every night, she'd sleep in his head
smearing soot, stamen, cocoa on cotton cream;

his fingertips on skin faint as the trace of insect legs
or the first dawn-light on closed eyelids.

II. Our Lady of the Rock

And the angel of the Lord found her by a fountain
of water in the wilderness, by the fountain in the way
to Shur. And he said, Hagar, Sarah's maid, whence
camest thou and whither wilt thou go?

GENESIS 16.7-8

It wakes Sarah – the same bright yellow dawn
          as on the boat that brought her
     and coaxed her, onto deck to watch
white cliffs, the horizon.

She opens windows wide over the street:
          these jostling roofs, the abbey:
     spiked towers on the hill, its shrieks
out-stripping the swallows.

To stretch above and reach to wry brook-beds,
          is watching close: a man's step
     (the bats squeal evening and night:
always the flapping wings).

The café where her sister sits; Hagar
          at table, her black hair tied
     round her head, coiled in feint of sleep,
proving her white bare neck.

Notice the flash of white cotton, the glare
          at the window and how these
     shutters close. The serene dun lulls,
gifts Sarah's head with coils.

          Then Sarah at table, still the cherub.
Their mother watched her mouthing,
          jawing in the choir's front row.
          Hagar gets up to leave;

turning her face to the hotel she finds
          inside the room is clean and
     bare – the book and window agape.
Past the abbey, the grass,

grows wild, long strands caught in cross-hatched breezes,
          tips swirling: black and white dots
     between TV channels. Angels
climb ladders to the spire.

Sitting cross-legged on the stone floor, dozing
like Jacob, cold was creeping
through her dress. The last mural is
crumbling: a woman

lifting dish to boy's mouth and the other
watching with bow and bright shaft.
'Hagar and Sarah,' he said in English
and the rhyme of steps followed her outside.

III. Blodeuwedd

Pan yr wyf i'n agos at y tŷ yn y tywyll, yr wyf i'n gweld
y mae'r ffenestr yn oleugerth a phan yr wyf i'n cyrraed,
yr wyf i'n ymdeithio i mewn i hyrddio fy hunan
ar y carped coch, gwresog a meddal o flaen y tân.
Here in the house, red and yellow flowers are still
bunched passive in my basket leaves stuck together
with the wet. I still pick my way down
the black mud path, rip through the hedge to pick
the finest buds from Mr Lloyd's flower bed, but
tonight I met the boy I chased; he held sticks
in his hands until he saw me, my arms full –
dry twigs strewn over wet earth, fingers in damp hair.
But I like this house: the *gwres*, carpet *a'r defaid*
yn galw tu allan. Yr wyf i'n pigo deilen o un coes,
yn sefyll, yn edrych i mewn y cwpwrdd am siswrn.
In the window's black, a face peers in:
my husband, his muddied forehead burst
into a criss-cross of lines his worries stuck
in folds of skin. He frowns so
he has an old man's face. He's *dicllon,*
ond yr wyf i'n dal trimio'r blodau gwlyb.
           Outside, the sheep in the barn
are mewing; my husband comes in: dead owlets
in a metal bucket. He notices the flowers
under the lamp on the table.
'Mae'n un ffordd i fyw.'
                'It's a way of making a living.'

Blodeuwedd: literally 'flower face'; the story from the Mabinogion tells
of a woman made of flowers who later is punished by Gwydion, the magician,
and turned into an owl. See page 88 for translations.

IV. Bedlam Bazaar
The Emperor

The castle surrounded by houses and traffic,
half buried crown in mud of its people.
The tourists who litter the green with their bodies,
snapping up farmhouses, princes and priests.

The well in the square was long since covered over;
the tree was cut down where a monk was once hung.
In the houses they turn back damp cloth from the window
where skaters slide back up the deep frozen river.

We carry the weight, the craft of our people,
to the port and the market where grey fingers delve.
We carry the city, the houses and steeples
to the port and the market where we sell ourselves.

And that man in the pub who sells pills for arthritis;
and the sheep you found leaking blood in the lane,
and the *mamiaith* that sings on the house on the corner,
to gramophone records that stick and then stutter.

And the tramp's gnarled toes will grow rotten in leather;
and the acid bath, warm in the depths of the cellar,
and governments rise from those broken slum houses,
from the nerve that beats deep under feet on the pavement.

We carry the weight, the craft of our people,
to the port and the market where grey fingers delve.
We carry the city, the houses and steeples
to the port and the market where we sell ourselves.

V. The Clarinet Player

United by the hierophant, we bridge the sacred mysteries, bow to God's mouth.

'I don't know whether to love or loathe the clarinet player,'
he replied at last. 'At midnight, notes inch through walls
from two doors down, wing through air, patter on the windowpane;
her room – full of clutched possessions: champagne flutes,
> a wooden cupid,
> that yellow dress thrown
on the chair, underwear in glistening layers.
Before the concert, a bright scent in the hall: her hair tied up
in tight, little knots so the bloom of her cheek was free to breathe.
She straightened her back in the midst of the music,
her lips parted and blew life in wood: busy streets,
> a mouthful of teeth,
> the yellow dress thrown.
Music and light pitched from cracks under a door.'

VI. The Jewel-box

Herr K. is to be put in place of your father just as he was in
the matter of standing beside your bed. He gave you a jewel-case;
so you are to give him your jewel-case.

> SIGMUND FREUD,
> *Case Histories I*

I become a closed garden, collapsing castle. Yet hear that!
A knock at my crag: a buzzard's reach of nesting thatch,
brim of nails, bone or teeth. Remember the rivet grip and
the ram. My lover is a pauper to whom I gift my fingers
as music for speaking and silence; yet I am a soldier.
I do not beg for fleshly talk, a luxurious bed: muscling
in a square room, I bring love. Who is that there ravelling in
the closed garden? The ram, who will have my purse, brings
a pearl and a boy knock-knocks at humming piano keys.
My love is the thrum of brown nightingale, for he sings
the bell of me and recalls begging entry. *Who shall enter?*
Remember the widow: she, of knitting or dam, spindles
at my door. But who will come in? My love knocks at pearl
and purse; yet I am a square room with such long lessons
in my fingers, tokens of paupers. But still a knock-knock
at eagle's defiance, at a buzzard's reach. Now will you not come in?
A pauper without, I tap at doorframes and windowpanes.

VII. Our Lady of Situations

*Things which have once been in contact with each other
continue to act on each other at a distance after the contact
has been severed.*

                                    J.G. FRAZER

On the overnight train, she waits, breath damp; her body
is an avalanche, one arm cascades into the aisle, splays fingers:
She closes her eyes: small hands grasp a book.

> *That balcony swung above the
> square. Mont Blanc. Mountains
> I   scaled   in   cable   car,
> overlooking   my   mother;
> the ground holding beneath us
> through   the   open   door.*

On the plateau, she fell in her red snow suit, sank to stand an imprint of herself
      in the snow.
Cold deep to her knees, her mother's bitter fingers and her father ducked into
      snow. More than this:
the balcony over the square and the evening light that glared the roofs red.

By morning, ice crags topple with a breath. She squints, fingers the page with
      gloves –
in heat she covers all skin but her high cheek – and buds from Sofia will fade
      to leaf.
Outside, silver young olive trees, brown leathered canopies: stalls in green villages
      sell great jars.

On glimpsing the sea, she pins her hair tight round her head
and is glad when the train shunts into Istanbul. She heaves
her bag on her back and goes alone into the city to begin.

VIII. Our Lady of Snows

O meichti ladi owr leding – tw haf
at hefn owr abeiding...

IEUAN AP HYWEL SWRDWAL

You pass an old woman crossing the bridge
and offer me a brown paper parcel;
your outstretched arm is the frozen river.

Inside the paper, a woollen coat, thick
and red, its buttons glint synthetic gold
at the shuffling old woman crossing the bridge.

Frozen winters at home, the cold blossom
of snow: knees blue and purple from skating
when the river froze to an outstretched arm.

At night my mother's voice reading aloud
and the window that never closed rattling
above village women crossing the bridge.

Pulling on the red coat over my dress
is a consolation and I gaze for fish
beneath the frozen river, an outstretched arm.

I must wait for some conclusion to this,
our meeting, some signal that I can go.
I am the woman crossing the bridge over an outstretched arm, the frozen river.

IX. Hecate

Upon the corner of the moon
There hangs a vap'rous drop profound.
I'll catch it ere it come to ground.
WILLIAM SHAKESPEARE.

Here, I have a west facing room above a white tree,
and on the shelves are jars of pickles: eyes, fingers and ears
– an ice cream van clangs out tunes in the street below.

Those summers at the hotel, the yellow light of dawn bright
as electricity. I woke at six with my grandmother long before the guests were up
and sat on the back doorstep eating bread and cheese.

In the hotel garden, I scrubbed at spider webs, mould
and spattered dirt on the chair legs. A bird flew up from long grass
with a great flapping of wings rustling like newspaper.

I take a finger from a jar and slice it open for the bone;
a hand that once opened its fingers to pluck an apple
or orange, felt its cool weight of a juggling ball.

My grandmother gave me an orange on Christmas Eve
and sent me up the long flight of wooden stairs;
that night, I dreamed of the white enamel bathtub with animal feet.

We often sat in it together and segments of oranges floated
on the surface. 'Eat up,' she said but a breeze rushed in
from the hallway where you stood at the door.

To discover your thoughts, I take an eye
and pressing my nail into the place where the eyeball
met the brain, I open my mouth for the white globe.

That flesh texture on my tongue is almost
like eating a lychee; I spit the hard centre in my palm:
brown shiny bean, black pupil.

I had short hair as a child unlike the women who passed through
the hotel, women with curls tumbling out from under their wide brimmed hats,
and when I met you I wanted long hair that we could both suffocate in.

My grandmother's favourite – the cape gooseberry that relieves regret;
peel back the veined paper shell to reveal the bitter fruit
fat as an orange blister: bite from the stem and swallow it whole.

X. My Grandfather

gripped his thigh when the line of planes took
off, his knees bunched in
the rear gunner cockpit. Light pierced the dense
thicket of noise, so
when he peered through that misted glass,
he glimpsed
a face in the plane parallel; the cast
of his friend was a
pale print lit for an instant and
then gone.

The drone of the engine continued its
constant humming and
he was rocking in time with the engine's
perpetual growl.
He thought of the dead at home when the plane
flew over a map
of lights – the German town they had been sent
to bomb and the flash
and growl when the city was hit soon faded
in the engine's drone.

On the ground, he queued in the line of men
waiting to draw a wide, white tick next to
their names; by one name, no mark:
a black space on the board filmed with dust:
smoke in the night sky.

XI. Love Song for His Mother

Woman is an object, sometimes precious, sometimes harmful,
but always different.

OCTAVIO PAZ

He thinks of her as a series of objects,
like the badly fitting glove she left on a bench
in the city park; on returning there was
only that bench and the empty green.

Her language conjured long-tailed birds
and there in the beak of the word something bright.
In the front of taxis, she used a hand mirror
first to check her lipstick, then angling it

to catch him in the back seat, or that candle she lit
when the lamp blacked out with all the light in the city;
the key he glimpsed in the bosom of her blouse,
a heavy chunk of metal for box or door.

Even after she was gone, he passed her place each day:
something white in a high window – not a face,
but the white belly of a pigeon beating its wings
against the pane in the boarded-up house.

XII. Canopy

*Odin hung upside down for nine nights on the world tree and
at the end was granted the wisdom of the runes.*

He's late today when he brings the news – the click
of my grandfather's jaw where he hung limp
on his seat belt, his nose broken on the front dashboard.
One cheekbone is higher, his face skewed.

The head that tilts, the hands that thaw in his lap.
We used to sit and watch, even on chill evenings
when he'd hang baskets of red flowers neat on their hooks.
Hands, bark of trees speckled with lichen.

Palms that would pat, leaven the earth's crumble.
At the window his arms hang from his shoulders;
we must wait for a sign watching flowers grow.
You say you knew his hands when they were young.

Come in where my grandmother pours the tea:
hot water and leaves lick the side of the cup.
See my grandfather's napkin hung neatly round his neck
– his uneven shoulders; so he watches trees.

XIII. A Small Unit of Time

For that which is born, death is certain...Therefore
grieve not over that which is unavoidable.
THE BHAGAVAD–GITA

Some nights he'd make a mug of hot chocolate
before we went to his room: the kitchen
that always smelled of roast beef, milk in a mug
and the microwave timer ticking down.

I stared at the digits, dismantled them with my eyes,
numbers that emerged and vanished in the flash of lines.
Milk bubbling, the mug on the table where I sat,
the jar of chocolate and stacked ladle.

I stirred it slowly until the milk turned brown
and the steam was coated with that chalked smell.
Trying to drink it slowly, I ran my tongue
round the mug's rim, placed it on the mantel.

'Haven't you finished it yet?' He waited
lounging in front of the TV, legs straddling.
I read the TV guide, filled the time with my voice;
by then it was too late and he had to drive me home.

This poem does not contain the letter 'P'.

XIV. Lonesome City Dweller

How poor are they that ha' not patience.
What wound did ever heal but by degrees?
WILLIAM SHAKESPEARE

She is the plain, the eclipse and ruined city
where we walk at dusk through these riverbank tunnels;
that rose in her buttonhole: a tomb for wrestlers.

On the skyline, the dome swells over flatter roofs,
tug-boats on the river and bright windows:
she is the moon and the pavement and stepping shoes.

The riverside cluttered with stalls selling books;
that puppet show features a wooden gentleman
with a bowler hat (from here darkness blooms).

She walks with me in the emptiness of crowds,
while I read that stranger's smile, this woman's frown:
I am the eye and the window and outstretched palm.

Earlier in the café we overheard talk
of her home country, more gossip of strife and death
and she stirred her long drink into a thunderstorm.

Under the bridge she is thinking of her mother:
that crossing in the ruins, that city pocked by gunshot.
She is the dark and desert and memory:
its walls invisible, its boundaries the sky.

XV. The Secret

A peculiar symptom in those poisoned by Belladonna is the complete loss of voice.
MEDICAL DICTIONARY

Dyma'r Wyddfa a'i chriw; dyma lymder, a moelni'r tir.
They said: *Why do you want to go to that place? There is nothing*
to see. And I said: *But I like its name. It means 'snow' and 'death'.*
It has something to do with the colours of red and green. So,

they were talking about the war, the table still uncleared
in front of them. Centuries of hate divide the Severn channel
from the Welsh. Far away, dark before the shining exit gates,
some place was waiting, its features unrecognisable.

I was born in the place on a slope few see that falls westwardly
like the feel of a pulse in the dark when I stay up all night.
Its name – how impossible! A piece of grass on the tongue
kidneys slipped from silk or striding the night for speckled eggs.

But me your work is not the best for – nor your love the best,
nor able to commend the kind of work for love's sake.
I am a settler East of the River, but back I have come
wintering in a dark without window at the heart of the house.

XVI. The Citadel

Security is the mother of danger and the grandmother of destruction.
THOMAS FULLER

From *tŵr* to eye-span, I forge a space:
castell of stone, cement and mangonel
or *coron* half buried by mud and daub.

My *tŵr* spans the eye, forges a place
besieged by *Branwen*; each ripe bird-call: a plum.
The fortress for an *ysbryd*, a green lady,

who opposed invasion by *bytholwyrdd*:
a *coron* half buried by legions of pines.
Those *teithwyr* stare up at my battlements

besieged by *brain*: each stark bird-cry – a crack.
The south tower slides to sixty degrees,
submits to invasion by *bytholwyrdd*.

I slump to reedy *Gororau*, greening glades.
Teithwyr keep watch on my battlements:
Brân's empty beak in the midday sun.

The tower slumps under sixty canon.
Distawrwydd in birdsong lost to a century
will mark the slump to *Gororau*, pining glades.

My *tŵr* and moat-span will forge a place
for *Brân*: his talons clawless in midday sun,
his hushed crowsong lost to a history.

Tŵr: a tower; *castell:* a castle; *coron:* a crown; *Branwen:* white crow (a princess in the Mab-inogion); *ysbryd:* a spirit or ghost; *bytholwyrdd:* evergreen; *teithwyr:* travellers; *brain:* crows; *Gororau:* borders (the Marches); *Brân:* a crow (Branwen's brother in the Mabinogion); *distawrwydd:* silence.

31

XVII. Epithalamion

These stars, the Pleiades, guard our spirit and seed,
become home for the Dakota's fathers.

Infinity

Street lamps brighten, the sky fades orange;
stars are dull, become a clue to laws
of other times, relics: the stone walls
found under Antarctica, pyramids that spelled
the stars of Orion's belt, tunnels burrowed
in stone to gaze at planets;
regret is round as a circle and can be worn as a bracelet,
but is deeper than the lake in a brown-headed wood
where they dive at night not finding the bottom

Crown

When night-fall drapes the horizon
the singing begins; first in the stars,
the sniff of a feathery nose,
a hunt in night-beds and cells,
then in the erotic charge of one
the hungering desire of the North Star's orbit,
that outstretched love of moon for water;
for in the love of women, the love of men
each must gift the other's head with stars.

XVIII. The Orphic Principle
A Poem for Three Voices

pp   Yr un a wnaeth gwae dan f'ais, cyffyrddwch sŵn fy llef.
mf   Yr un a wnaeth gwae dan f'ais, cyfyrddwch sŵn fy llef.
f   Yr un a wnaeth gwae dan f'ais, cyfyrddwch sŵn fy llef.

f   Power
is the virgin
who, like a dynamo,
turns men to mastered particles,
voltage.

pp   Garaf ac y gerais.
mf   Garaf ac y gerais.
f   Garaf ac y gerais.

pp   At night, I ride home:
question marks of lamps arc or
sickle. The train screams.

pp   Blodyn y gwynt ydw i.
mf   Blodeuyn yr eira ydw i.
f   Ffrwyth y taranau ydw i.

mf   I choose my clothes with care to make me invisible,
pick out blues and greys, soft materials, so
I seethe in darkness, transparent under streetlamps.

Passers by never see me, only that strange sense of light
sparkling on fine hair; something brushes an elbow, a knee:
I choose the wing of a skirt to make me invisible.

Night is less cluttered, its tastes are more pungent;
voices spin through the rain from open windows
seething in darkness, transparent under street lamps.

Here, I could be the roaring of wind that makes leaves blink,
but I think I'm more like the moon that fades with the dawn;
it chooses daylight to make itself invisible.

Even more than this, I am the rush of cold air and
smell of soot in train carriages passing through a tunnel;
I seethe from darkness, transparent under fluorescent lamps.

33

The fiddle of fingers on beads, a lit cigarette,
a mouthful of teeth; he gets in a taxi and it drives away.
I choose my clothes with care to make me invisible,
seething in darkness, invisible under light.

pp   Yr un a wnaeth gwae dan f'ais, cyffyrddwch sŵn fy llef.

pp   Yr un a wnaeth gwae dan f'ais, cyffyrddwch sŵn fy llef.
mf   Yr un a wnaeth gwae dan f'ais, cyffyrddwch sŵn fy llef.

pp   Yr un a wnaeth gwae dan f'ais, cyffyrddwch sŵn fy llef.
mf   Yr un a wnaeth gwae dan f'ais, cyffyrddwch sŵn fy llef.
f   Yr un a wnaeth gwae dan f'ais, cyffyrddwch sŵn fy llef.

The three voices in this poem are defined by dynamic indications in music, so pp stands for *pianissimo* meaning 'very quietly', mf stands for *mezzo-forte* meaning 'medium loud' and f stands for *forte* meaning 'loudly' or 'strong'.

XIX. She

(after T.H. Parry Williams)

I arrived with the last snow of spring, erred across
to burrow in mountains (too small to be a loss).

A rough patch of skin on the sole of a foot, her clutter
causes slight dismay to those who believe in order.

Trace the bones of a country buried deep in her, or
grin at litany and nation and a native's core.

Her lovers are unmentionable; the dull drone
to fill her emptiness: the whine of a trombone.

The muzzle of red light loses its bite far from herds
of dumb animals – extremists bleat empty words.

Wind rakes hair, lacerates clothes screaming over rough terrain
at the mountain top. My imagination: a steam train.

Heaviness of cloud tumbles over land,
fields raked like people's pockets. So I scan

the horizon for the house where I was born: here
native voices tucked in brickwork are just as clear;

her hair nets my imagination, her roots
wrap my bones, my skull pinned underfoot.

XX. Metropolis

*History will tumble down and break into atoms
in the lap of the twentieth century.*
JULES MICHELET

They hide in the house, turn back the black cloth
    that covers the window; outside people
cross the shivering river, frozen moths
    lured to tall buildings, power's bloody steeples.

She stabs a potato at the table:
    the weight of a heart, her mother would say
and dig her fingers in earth. She disables
    the organ for the microwave's display.

Back from trenches, he sleeps upstairs all day;
    his toes turned blue and putrid in his boots:
the green river through the wood to the bay
    that napalm and petrol pollute.

The title of pilots they couldn't shoot
    named after the Middle Age Mongol fleet
that folded into waves on its route
    to Japan: sacrificed in light and heat.

'Blitzkrieg,' he said and spoke of incomplete
    flesh upon cheek upon skin upon bone.
'Operation Overlord': earth and peat
    of Normandy: 'Operation Sea Lion'

and at night, the roses and dandelions
    burn down with the glass palace; we repeat
the crumbling of Babel from word to bone:
    fat ambition and frail bodies compete.

Down the road, a man has a bath to heat
    acid and on the procession route
Princip loiters in the crowd among fleets
    of news carts. SILENT STAR ARBUCKLE SHOOTS

HIS LAST SCENE – the paper precious loot
    of scandal is only ever kept at bay
by human interest; small child with polished boots:
    9 YEAR OLD VIOLINIST PLAYS HALL TODAY.

We'd go down to Yasgur's farm for the stark display
of women's bodies, or clubs that disabled
the senses with cabaret and hearsay:
men or women dancing with chairs, on tables.

Outside, placards wave under the steeples,
desires crushed to powdered moth.
Beers or plants ease minds of grey people
who hide inside and turn back the black cloth.

XXI. Trade

Now the oceans
are mapped, we sail deep
into strange continents where people
are small and grey, where most never leave
the parish of their birth. Up the hill from the port,
I rub at the window of the shop with a soaped cloth;
Mister Vasquez leans in the doorway, his soft body bulges
under his shirt. I stop for a moment to look down the hill at
the white sails of ships; the boats come in full of sugar, flax
and cotton from countries that no one has visited. I pronounce
a name, try to imagine its people: flax and linen from *the Baltic*,
oranges from *Greece*, *Colombian* physalis. When the window is
clean, I scrub with a broom at the pavement, at the red dust
caught in the grouting, the red dust smudged on hands and
faces, settled over clothes. He yawns in the doorway and
as I polish the black tiles on the shop front, I dream
of the marketplace: green and purple vegetables,
silver strung beads, blue bottles of elixir and
medicinal powders made by a woman
living high on a hill above boats
sailing in, the port.

THE GREATER SECRETS
A 21 DAY ROUND

The object, I could first distinctly view,
Was tall, straight trees, which on the water flew;
Wings on their sides, instead of leaves, did grow,
Which gathered all the breath the winds could blow:
And at their roots grew floating palaces,
Whose outblowed bellies cut the yielding seas.

JOHN DRYDEN

THE GREATER SECRETS: 20 DAY AZTEC ROUND

DAY 1:	Day of *Cipactli*, the Great Lizard	*Migration*
DAY 2:	Day of *Ehécatl*, the Wind	*Ten Fingers, Ten Thumbs*
DAY 3:	Day of *Calli*, the House	*Calendar*
DAY 4:	Day of *Cuetzpallin*, the Small Lizard	*Lizard*
DAY 5:	Day of *Coatl*, the Snake	*Serpent*
DAY 6:	Day of *Miquiztli*, Death	*The Flying Bed*
DAY 7:	Day of *Mázatl*, the Deer	*Meon Hill*
DAY 8:	Day of *Tochtli*, the Rabbit	*Quarry*
DAY 9:	Day of *Atl*, Water	*Fish-eye*
DAY 10:	Day of *Izcuintli*, the Dog	*Anaglypta*
DAY 11:	Day of *Ozomatli*, the Monkey	*My Dress Hangs Here*
DAY 12:	Day of *Malinalli*, the Grass	*My Convent Skull*
DAY 13:	Day of *Acatl*, the Reed	*Everything Under the Earth*
DAY 14:	Day of *Océlotl*, the Jaguar	*Saboteur*
DAY 15:	Day of *Cuahtli*, the Eagle	*Yield*
DAY 16:	Day of *Cozcacuahtli*, the Buzzard	*The Long-tailed Bird*
DAY 17:	Day of *Ollin*, Movement	*Collision*
DAY 18:	Day of *Técpatl*, the Knife	*Assassin*
DAY 19:	Day of *Quiahuitl*, the Rain	*The Guitar*
DAY 20:	Day of *Xóchitl*, the Flower	*Journeying*

DAY 1: **Migration**

The native language
is dead as Esperanto.
Creaking cicadas
remember and sing trilling
consonants among

      fertile Spanish groves. At last,
      the birds will migrate
      to wet forests, their heads bald.
      Bleak feathers fall on
      the cities and countryside.

In jungle they perch
on the black body of a great lizard:
cocodrilo sleeps
with birds on its pitted back:
a survival pact.

Vultures cry: cipactli,
            cipactli,   cipactli.

My country, *cilfach*
cefn, uneasy annexe
to an upright land.
This country see-saws between
two continents. Here

      is the house where I was born
      and here the school house.
      My people working the land
      for its sweet composts,
      grafting pear and apple boughs:

peren ac afal.
Grandfather's empty birdcage:
the long plumed bird
that he coveted and kept
for his own is dead.

The crow's song: crafangau
          crafangau   crafangau.

DAY 2: **Ten Fingers, Ten Thumbs**

Heaven guide thy pen to print thy sorrows plain,
That we may know the traitors and the truth.

WILLIAM SHAKESPEARE

I set out on my journey, a woman, until turning from the dark car window,
the driver's seat was empty. Somewhere in the field, a man was hunting, his pupils
the centre for the hands of a clock. At the house, three albino twins sat with ears
to a gramophone whispering secrets *we won't want you here, we don't want you here*
Now, a woman, I carry sterile ghosts heavy on my back to winter solstice
when the earth is a snail withdrawn deep in labyrinthine shell – I travel onwards
to summer tempests when the sky is a humid tortoise shell, a taut down-turned bowl.
Here is the house of the jaguar drum, its people suffering every blow
in union; here is my mother, here my grandfather, his ears trained for the horn's blast,
for restlessness, for journeys. It began in the closed one of silence or let's say
it began in the pursed garden of watchful lips. It began with my grandfather
who saw, on leaning over the mine gate, the shaft fall as slate and decapitate
his mate's fingertips. Let's begin with England and dayschool, trips when the woollen
        hides
of farms muscled their way to lambs, tense milk, gums barking behind every locked door.
Later the removal van down the hill: my father's blue hand of forgetfulness.
I travel, a woman, on from the border of one country to yet another
with my ten toes finding footholds, my ten fingers and thumbs heaving their guilty load.
I aped the library that my vowels knew, the grandmother that my words had heard of:
bethma, gwreiddiau, madre, corazón. White twilight approaches but,
as woman, I must live as long as parrots do, moult like them and change my feathers.

DAY 3: **Calendar**

• • •

My gullet:
a snake pierced
by arrows.

• • • •

To lash by beast.
To slay by wind.
To strafe by flood.
To void by rain.

<u> • • </u>

Besieged, hated are our towns
and compounds ringed by cactus.
They play the conch shell and drum
at gates all night; not even
their lights tempt us from haven:
the chrysalis bud: a wick
that bursts wingspans of flame.

The Mayan people had a complex mathematical system and as Maria Longhena explains in
Maya Script, 'the simplest method was the use of dots for units and bars for the number
five'. The poems above are dedicated to the numbers three, four and seven, all of which
were sacred to the Maya.

DAY 4: **Lizard**

*A pre-clinical dopaminergic deficit precedes clinically
evident Parkinson's Disease by many years. An event
or process that ultimately results in disease may occur
or begin in youth.*

Sixty years ago paddling on the Gulf
the tar of black gold, mahogany docked
at port, its sap rich with schemes of money.

The girl on the pier points a long finger
from the flat Caye to the Caribbean.
Ashore, her house with the green porch.

A woman sings in Spanish in a house
further down; the father on the veranda
puts his pince-nez to his nose to look out to sea.

Leaves poke out from the centre of palms
like so many hands from the face of a clock.
I trail my boots in the dust, she in bare feet.

Later she traces an eye in the sand: sketch
of a window, mock of an Indian tattoo.
A broom leans at the corner of the house.

I run down the long pier in the dark and leap
– underwater blood moves in circles about my ears,
the seething coral, membranous as brains or red as coals.

I pull on a wet boot but something squirms to life,
a small green lizard emerges to streak the sand
and climb the side of the clapboard house

and to bend again over that sodden boot
is to feel the fine flexing of my spine,
to sense the heavy weight about my shoulders,
to taste the beetle that sits on my tongue.

44

DAY 5: **Serpent**

I was angry with my foe
I told it not, my wrath did grow
WILLIAM BLAKE

So we spent that first month near an orchard
where the fruit fell down for us to skin;
with teeth, fingers and knives we burrowed in,
we tunnelled in to be hated and tarred.
For women did not know our faces
and tension was keener in villages:
the elders all dead, young men prone to rages
tender and fearful for their birthplaces.
The grudge in them grew till it burst flower
and for us to pick that fig from the tree
was sunlight and cut glass, its trickery
setting the fruit trees ablaze, the tongue sour.
The apple and gun in these hands are mine
and dead is the foe who sees them shine.

DAY 6: **The Flying Bed**

We only come to sleep, we only come to leave.
It's not true, it's not true, that we come to live on the land.
MEXICAN FOLKSONG

Beneath my lover's face, there lies a skull;
at night his chin casts shadows on his breast.
Beneath Judas' skin, a ribcage, birdcage.

In bed, I dream of a dead child; my womb
is a withdrawing snail: it wanes like the moon.
The Virgin's face reveals a grinning skull.

The doctor unpacks my shattered organ,
and says my youthful folly is to blame.
The saint's fingers were white under the flesh.

Still the reckless pump, the purple machine dies
and my violated orchid bone remains.
In the distance, skyscrapers grow erect, wheels turn.

Did you see a stranger with a long grey switch,
his iron shovel mining for a coin or trick?

I am broken ramparts, a nunnery tumbled;
for like the Ploughboy at Alveston, I see
the black dog and ride by tree-trunks
on intricacies of leaves: the sign
of the cross at my throat and ear.
Where I tend the slopes and hedges,
banks and cornfields near Meon,
my trouncing hook juts out an extra digit.

Herbs so hearty: Devil's Parsley.
Shepherd's Purse: Devil's Curse.

I am an apple bitter of rind: I fall
seedless. Yet I would be the Woodsman
stripping bark to bristling choke, or
piercing vegetable matter to a white eye.
At night I hear the owlish, hooting hounds,
the feathery sniffing of their noses,
the bright clink of claws in the lane:
the Ploughboy's red-eyed guardian mastiff.

Leaves in the lap: Devil's Nightcap.
Nightingale sing: Devil's Plaything.

Leaves that die on the boughs sound out
the sea on shingle; here the hound hangs
by its white eye, the fields dug with toads.
I feel the node of every pitchfork point
and lie beneath the dank brook-bed
binding the Devil to his own delight.
Such a long lesson in learning
how to wear my sex like a jewel.

On Meon Hill, the Devil dropped his load
by the lane that runs along the turnpike road.

DAY 8: **Quarry**

These stars that you call the Pleiades are the fruit
of the rabbit breeding and multiplying.

At night, I follow footprints, the five beans of each toe,
and the long loaf of the foot. The war-flowers are stained:
I follow the eye of each toe: the moon is the skull
of a bleeding rabbit, its pock – all that these people
have lost. I follow the flame of each toe, its branding
of soft earth. That is all that they answer to our breath:
they herald the moon's pock, the eye of a rabbit skull.
They watch those forest-soldiers who hack the dropping eye
of butterfly wings, who scrub the Z-like scar that bleeds
the softened bark. When stars fade to breath, the sun races
its blunt hooves through the wet forest horning and dappling
the blinking dead in their long loaf of flowery death.

DAY 9: **Fish-eye**

If you prick us do we not bleed?
WILLIAM SHAKESPEARE

If each lie or tongue were pricked with fish hooks –
those grey eels, these sleek grey sentinels
patrolling such river waters and each grievance
sharpens a tooth: a turned shoulder or twist
of the lips or laughter, an eye's movement,
a hand withdrawn, pinched flesh, a heavy step.
A fish-eye is not like. Purblind infinity,
that never-ending propulsion and withdrawal:
these flat hands, this strata and rigging,
a green breath, my spiny affection,
such moist passion, a white baited throat.
The reel will spin until the line is hung:
I've set the bait to catch a lie or tongue.

DAY 10: Anaglypta

See if I loved you, it was for your hair;
now that you're bald, I don't love you any more.
1940s MEXICAN SONG

And her skin fits round her body
like badly hung wallpaper in a damp house,
bubbles and cracks emerging each day
to blemish mirrors and glassy surfaces.

Just as the leaves of trees turn orange
falling in gutters and drains
so her flesh yellows, her hair falls
in clumps that stick to her clothes.

At restaurants, liquid dribbles from
her eyes, nose, the corner of her mouth;
her stomach bulges with its precious load
of bilious gas, raw acid, fat.

Staggering on the slick avenue,
she appeals to this woman, that man.
A long, empty shape in the gutter:
a dead-head full of withered seeds.

DAY 11: My Dress Hangs Here

on a washing line over the city;
a woman's flag, threaded with lashes
of eyes, of windows, desire and pity,
measures time with its tightening seams.

It is the receiver where I listen
to faint breathing at the end of the line,
or the bridge I cross from myself in search
of a dull silhouette in the green river.

My dress is a queue of women each jostling
the other to inch forward a small step
or it is an artifact on display
photographed in grey newspaper clippings.

Passive, maternal, childish, aspiring,
crazed, ablaze, frank, enraged,
broken, resistant, grateful, appealing,
plaid, patchwork, clue – my dress.

In Aztec mythology, *Ozomatli*, the great orator, sculptor and
writer of glyph was lured into the tree by the jealous brothers
and transformed into an ape, a monkey god.

DAY 12: **My Nunning Skull**

We have gathered vast populations incapable of free survival, insulated
From the strong earth, each person in himself helpless, on all dependent.
ROBINSON JEFFERS

To remember I invoke the girth and grit
of castle walls – those brute watchmen –
where a door discloses a trap, that reveals
a window, that opens a drawbridge.

Like the frozen moat, my ice is stubborn
but thick enough to carry the weight of men.
In spring and summer, the common thrush
and nightingale beg an opening.

To look, I lie the half-turn of a drape,
the strap of heather to breast or collar.
The perfume ran on my hands and nails:
scent wet on the blunt key in the lock.

Whether to refrain or refrain from love?
Behind the door, the beam held only a hawk;
its beak spired to spiral staircase leading nowhere:
the feathery shriek sounded your absence.

DAY 13: Everything under the Earth

At the border, scold's bridles block mouths;
we, officials, drop our paperwork
from a high platform so it tumbles
to grass, to colours of cenote.
It will find the collapse of limestone:
underground brawny water beds where
rock buries spiny fossils, watching
itself be rock, wrapping itself round
cracks and fissures, knowing its colours

intimately. It crushes the voice
of by strata; it seals the mouth
of by lamina. Water from cracks
drops like the word made manifest from
a human mouth or something bright from
the beaks of long-tailed parrots; paper
falls to the collapse of a people:
a sink hole of lime crushes the word
made manifest from such high platforms.

DAY 14: **Saboteur**

*Silent jaguar, bloody his mouth and red his claws,
a slayer, devourer, killer of men.*

The market stalls set up in the square;
the grey door of the church stands open:
on the steps, an argument –
a man carrying bill posters points a long finger
at the woman with broom.

At one stall, the boy from number 22
sets out parts of radios, engines, TV sets;
he can take a TV apart in ten minutes
but the tedium of putting each part in its place,
returning each screw, routed wires, metal.

The grocer has set out the fruit on a table;
he picks up a lemon, holds it like a bomb.
The man on the steps is shouting;
his bill posters fall, are blown a little way
before they stick to the wet pavement.

That man who skirts the corner of the church
holding a briefcase under his arm, that figure
in spectacles who crosses the square
and drives away to infect the city:
a woman and child walk home down grey streets with a bag of lemons.

DAY 15: **Yield**

When the pumping heart is torn away, the eagle carries
that prickly fruit to the sun.

And they meet with a sense of height and danger
as if stood together on the stairwell
of a skyscraper: the fire below
whispering words like *trap* and *parchment* and *panic*.

Pressing her forehead against his cheek
is leaning on a window pane – the long drop below.
They close the door as smoke fills the room
and lie down in the heart of a crumbling building

Just as the blustering folds of trees speak a language,
mimic the sea, so do his ears, mouth, eyelashes
and his softest parts: flames shiver in reveries of wood.
Tu cuerpo alegre, tus luminosos ojos.

His fingers on her body tighten the strings of her.
She whispers another language to goad him, soothe him.
In the smoulder of her skin is a music
faint as the trickle in grass after a rainstorm.

Under the flesh, the ribcage, birdcage: never before
have they felt this singeing of the ribs and spine.
When the building falls away, two tin hearts leap up –
stones thrown up over water, birds arcing through space.

DAY 16: **The Long-tailed Bird**

Our defeat was always implicit in the victory of others;
our wealth has always generated our poverty by nourishing
the prosperity of others.

> EDUARDO GALEANO.

Citizens, come running! We can put it out!
Bring your pots brimming. Bring your jars of water.
These swift flames singe woodwork, our farmers' tillers.
It began far away and surged to the sky,
advanced against these walls, houses of boatmen.
Flooded homes yielded to paths of water-birds.

Days before on the lake's shore, they found a bird.
A passer-by clamoured: *O children, watch out!*
A grey crane trapped in the nets of the boatmen,
who fish the lake and praise the city waters.
Children, where can I hide you under this sky?
And what of the land? The green maize and tiller?

The hour was noon, but the bird's brow, ploughed or tillered
with glass, mirrored stars and evening song-birds.
The weathered goddess was keening to the sky;
she marshalled lances and arrows, threw spears out
against tidal winds. At the brink of water,
we captured them with longboats, those fierce boatmen.

The messengers returned with our proud boatmen.
They left the ships – the rudderless tiller –
left the galleons empty on the water.
Ashore, the wry wingspan of Blue Mockingbird
beat out each knife-stab and sword-stroke: life snuffed out.
They died blind, their grey eyes attending white skies.

We raised our muzzles to the wind, to ashen skies:
we brandished muzzles high, the scent of boatmen
wet on our jaws and mauls. *Why did you come out?*
It's too late for a God to take the tiller.
Out came the dancers feathered by hummingbird;
a drummer beat the ebb and flux of water.

Corpses in the rushes! Death in the water –
ripe as corn! Corpses in the reeds: ripe as sky.
Beneath pale throats of magnificent frigatebirds,
we sliced off the arms of drummers and boatmen;
heads rolling were sunken treasure among the tillers:
in a raucous dance, our revels were stamped out.

We live on water and weeds, cry the boatmen.
Under burgeoning skies, we grasp the tiller.
The curse of long-tailed bird will never die out.

DAY 17: **Collision**

And then the strange room where the brightest light
Does not shine on the strange men: shines on me.
JOHN BERRYMAN

At dawn she falls from the centre of the world,
and by morning she no longer believes in fate.
Broken in the dawn, that indignant girl
of previous days, fearless in back-streets,
oblivious of men who stare; this girl
defaced, defrocked in the bleak light.
Those objects collected
from the busy night streets?
> *A key will unlock me.*
> *A toy car propels me.*
> *A silver hat-pin knits me.*

This young moon goddess rides the waxing crescent,
ignores the ground that quakes beneath her.

Distracted by a glint in the wet gutter,
she bends down to see an old woman's face;
she stoops too late to notice that man,
a freight train.
She looked up at the oncoming traffic
with surprise and some curiosity
as in dreams behind her huge oak door.
> *Wet painted words on bark.*
> *The gramophone's rebuke.*
> *Numbers substitute pupils.*

At dawn she recognises pain,
and by morning she cannot trust in fate.

DAY 18: **Assassin**

He leans over an old fashioned gramophone,
listens to the song stutter: *I can't – I can't –* ...
His hand fits his pocket comfortably,

his coat on the back of a chair, his hat
on the table and the case by the bed:
there, the woman he knew lies naked,

a towel thrown over her neck. Her head
is propped against the lion curtain – the trickle
of blood from her mouth is a ticker tape.

The curtain's rampant lions move him
to a sense of the silent stranger in the great coat
brandishing a club, the imperceptible man

in a bowler hat who grips a net. He turns to see
a group of people outside the window peering in
and behind them the peaks of mountains.

DAY 19: The Guitar

These beasts, celestial dragons conjure storms,
beat out such rhythms of blue bellied desire.

The young man braces a paper windmill
against red berries and green coffee-fields,
against that grey sky. The music he plays
fills us: revolving locomotion.
The folksong *Adelita* on the wind,
its notes – flat coins thrown in a pond or well.
Startled chords are the wings of a caught bird
or later, the easy spin of a wheel.
The movement of his fingers frees the hinge
of a longing spent and a rise and sigh.
His hands on the body tighten the strings
of a raucous dance and a frantic cry.
At last, hot rain begins to fall: we yield
to thunder and ride over coffee-fields.

DAY 20: **Journeying**

There is nothing like death in war,
nothing like flowery death
so precious to the Giver of Life:
far off I see it: my heart yearns for it.

AZTEC POEM

I know that corn is gritted for its germ,
and hear its tune sung loud with Spanish words.
I fear the golden beak that smudged the worm,
but miss refrains of whirring hummingbirds.
I pack my mother's fingers treading keys
and know that castle walls are a defence.
I have not climbed wet Guatemalan trees,
nor found in grief the cellars of offence.
I cannot know that man can hurt a hawk
nor sense the weave of sellers on the street.
I rest in sounds of words in mothers' talk
and quiver in the movement of the heat.
Through fields, I journey with my loaded pack,
to joy in rhyming footsteps, trip and track.

THE CURSE OF THE LONG-TAILED BIRD
AFTER BÉLA BARTÓK

*In colonial and neo-colonial alchemy, gold changes
into scrap metal and food into poison.*
EDUARDO GALEANO

ENTER MALINCHE

ENTRANCE
Enter Malinche, a tourist in these parts.
Enter the bluebeard, Cortés, his dark-secret heart:
the castle built on corpses, drawbridge and ramparts.

MALINCHE'S PROMISE
I will steady your numb castle
You and I will plumb the gold.
Walls may bluster, wind may burnish,
but we last here through the darkening.

CORTÉS' PROMISE
Nothing glitters in my castle.

Space-Time

Ordinary time appears to stand still on the horizon of a black hole.

Here is an island like a jewel or scarab
on the flat lagoon where herons wade.
They walk the circle of main-street from town-hall door
to town-hall gate and find that every pathway
leads to the waterfront where birds wing air-currents:
paths of filings in iron magnetism.

A buzzard of the Mexican highlands is drawn
by this feeding ground of turtle, shrimp and beetle:
gods that fell headlong from the sun's ripening course
to merge with the earthbound souls of the dead
and plague them invisibly for life and vigour,
the buzz of regret eclipsing the Milky Way.

She shows him the stars of the southern hemisphere
Here, the beekeeper wooing the hives with his charms,
and here, a lady – Obsidian Butterfly
spelled with stars, throwing arrows against tidal winds.
No more of the past, that which has always happened,
a remote island that jolts to life each day.

Lying on the pier, she puts an eye to the slats:
the lagoon's quiet pulse of bird foot or paddle
teaches her to hear and know a bird arced in space,
a pebble thrown up over water in the dark.
The sky will persist for a thousand years and I
will remain here young, in search of the Southern Cross.

SEVEN DOORS

MALINCHE'S DOUBT
I see seven doors all bolted,
but these portals must be opened.
For I hear a woeful sighing?
Each door laments with keening grief.

CORTÉS' DOUBT
No one sees what is behind them,
none will know the contents there.
Sweet Malinche, are you frightened?

MALINCHE
No for here! I have the key.

1. The Torture Chamber

The forces of public order are authorised to punish
with aid of appropriate weapons.

Malinche's eyes are split by needles,
    pocked by fat flies or by pin heads.
On her knees – the church, the burning –
    she collapses, killed by bullet.
Now she dies in forest townships
    taking blade-knives in her paunch –
the soldier trims her greased intestine
    to lithe sea worm, sodden weeds.

Exiting with shot to brain:
    her lumpen head is ball for game;
Zopilote, craven vulture,
    bills small bones, beaks the frame.
Under weighted-lids of town-wells,
    only nail and bone remains;
maculated ears are hanging
    for a thousand soldiers' fame:
anchored down in Lake Texcoco,
    she repays a country's blame.

OUTSIDE THE TORTURE CHAMBER

CORTÉS' QUESTION
Dear Malinche, are you frightened?

MALINCHE'S ANSWER
Look! The walls are bleeding, weeping.
Your castle walls are fouled by blood.
Now I see the wounds still opening
through the cracked and riven sunrise.
Now we sigh with doors and windows:
open up the second tomb.

2. The Armoury

Fortune favours the daring.

His indigenous vassals knew nothing of swords;
    eager to grasp the blade, they took the sharp edge
renting skin. All told were one hundred sailors,
    not many ladies, five hundred soldiers, sixteen horses,
a few harquebuses, muskets and ten bronze cannon,
    not counting Malinche with tongues of Spanish and Mexican.
Cacique by birth, her heart was a great muscle to dwarf mountains;
    only a fool would have thrown together such ingredients:
ripe chillies and meat fried for a ravening scent,
    the blackened cacao for the white fat of men's eyeballs.
Encouraged to choose, she could watch disenchanted
    softening chillies for their hungering, lingering smell.

OUTSIDE THE ARMOURY

CORTÉS' QUESTION
What do you spy through the doorway?

MALINCHE'S ANSWER
I see the death of kith and kin:
steel and armour, sword and dagger
parade the skulls of all my people.
Let me have the key you promised;
I do not falter in my mission.

3. The Treasury

Father a merchant, son a gentleman, grandson a beggar.

God and his majesty must be served by the finding of riches.
Understand the mountain with 4000 shafts, the temple:
a trove of coffee, indigo, gold and mineral, fruit and silver.
Night-dreams in Malinche's bed: dry crops swallow fat sheaves
or famished beasts bleed their swollen brothers.

Just to find the branches and fruit, you would do us harm.
Understand the guilt of bequest, the long-tailed bird,
a mirror in its crest – the dying sun predicts
that movement on the horizon; squadrons of warriors march
on Tenochtitlan and itch for gold like hungry swine.

OUTSIDE THE TREASURY

CORTÉS' QUESTION
See the lifetime of my bounty?

MALINCHE'S ANSWER
But each jewel is stained with blood.

CORTÉS' ANSWER
Not blood or gore my dear Malinche,
but the rust that comes with age.
If you're sickened by its colour,
wipe it clean or mist the pane.

4. The Garden

Is building on sugar better than building on sand?

Enter the monoculture.
Nature untroubled by commerce for centuries, favoured neither
coffee nor sugar, oil nor rubber above any other.
Over the years the indigenous woods found place at rich tables.
Mahogany lost its lustre in gilded furniture;
inked hearts of ebony rot in door frames of once splendid mansions:

Enter the industry.
Now in these banana republics, United Fruit and their ilk,
deport their departments for minerals, crops
and petroleum, bullets and bunches: the tree of hell.

AT THE GARDEN GATE

CORTÉS EXPLAINS
Behind this door a thing of beauty:
this garden full of flowers and posies.

LA MALINCHE'S WORM
This white rose: a sickening organ;
in its heart, there lies a worm.

CORTÉS' WINDOW
A heart that only begs your presence
at this freshly budding field
where you can survey my country:
know the bounty of a bride.

5. The Far Country

We had to get rid of a Communist government which had taken over.

Under the mountain were four thousand shafts,
now empty: the mossed peak slumps to dead stone,
                    abundant crags decline and topple.
Inside, they sweep out the seams with long brooms.

The blocked temple – its ambit from servitude to dynamo,
                    from powerhouse to slums –
exits flattened: a cathedral springs up in its place,
                    hanging gardens swell in its stead.

Dumb palm trees raise their heads at the prospect of cities;
sunflowers root themselves with cable,
the swift exchange between plant and bulb:
a letter sent to keep the bloodlines joined.

The spade founders, strikes the busy motor
entreating the dead earth. Flags raise their ruddy faces.
Sulphur gives way to frangipani, a loudspeaker opposes
                    her cupped hand.

OVERLOOKING THE FAR COUNTRY

CORTÉS EXPLAINS
My valley will be yours forever,
if you wish to stay with me.

MALINCHE'S QUESTION
In the distance, hoards of soldiers?

CORTÉS' ANSWER
Just wintry pines, these evergreens.

MALINCHE'S FEINT
Now I feel my body failing,
light diminishing to pin point.
Dark when I approach your pupil
like a train that comes to tunnel.

6. The Dark

There are no accomplices here other than you and I.
You as oppressor, I as liberator, deserve to die.

Here stood the train painted green with detail
in red: handles and window-frames.   Her head
declined on the mountain path, the earth off-
angle. Someone had died in Copper Canyon, but
leads *had* appeared – the cupboard's trapped cries,
girl-children tied with string, stashed in cases on
the luggage racks. The   carriage door slammed.
Zona de plagas.   *Next stop Loreto.*
At the next station, the carriage was filled:
peons, an American and his young wife.
A mother and her son searched cubicles.
The real detective was tied to the roof as the
black spot ahead grew from pinpoint to tunnel.

A MATCH

MALINCHE LISTENS
Hear that door, its sob, a sighing
in this grieving, deadening pool.

CORTÉS EXPLAINS
Here is water dear Malinche:
my dead wives' tears, their guilt as salt.
You discovered my best oceans –
corpsing secrets hide such wives.
You have been seduced by falsehood
and forgot the burgeoning peoples
struggling from low-lying throngs,
keeping safe their thought and habits
from the gutters to the forests.
I, the dry-plain that seduced you,
feigned a green oasis skull.

MALINCHE'S ANSWER
Spare me from your endless censure.
I will not wear this weighted gown.

CORTÉS' INTRODUCTION
Cease your prattling, stop your banter.
My crown appears: my seven wives.

7. The Wives

The sleeping woman slowly eats her midnight heart.

From here, you watch the door wedged shut, the gate to Costaguana.
Ready your shoulder and wait for the count of *A BEAT, B BEAT, C BEAT*
O is for travel, T – the train whistle, a Y in the tracks.
Z BEAT BEAT Now you will visit a burgeoning republic:
enveloped by treasure and deep in a sand bank, Sulaco,
night-flowering village, embraces your townhouse and courtyard.

From there, you heave the door aside: the attic room with glass ajar.
Rubbing at sill with flat of hand, you sit and pull in your knees
imbalanced by motes and moths gyrating – smoke from a blast.
Greening light in your squint: you look beyond the roofs for the plain,
haranguing dead forests for miles to the cliff tops. Then sea,
the black hulls of ships, the bones of sailors and reedy gull-cries.

Every day in the plaza your father digs and weeds roots of trees;
now you can see the top of his head, his back still labouring
by dry brook-beds; he waves a hand in the air that makes a fist.
Enraged, you turn inward to boards, slats and beams: humble tomb in
an attic's pyramid. *The window* – BEAT – *bangs against the frame.*
The women of Sulaco – BEAT – *suffer and are silent* – BEAT –

Eyes of a god could not fathom the depths of this dark room, where
nailed to hang over one sodden beam is waxen tarpaulin.
Blighted edges are nailed into floorboards to make a lean-to
or retreat: a tent. *Copper for atrophy: silver for teeth.*
Down there, you bend to a looped wire, one end nailed down, the other
enwrapping itself in a loose knot, a fraught noose.

Down there, not your father's trap for rats and birds. Not an ornament.
When you lean forward, palms flat on splintered wood: four wire nooses
one at each corner of the tent, one for each crook of the globe.
Measure the pitch. Gauge the four wire loops for two arms and two legs
and repeat: *four coils of wire for my two arms and my two legs.*
Now you crouch inside. You crouch very still.

THE PROCESSION OF WIVES

CORTÉS' INTRODUCTION
For your sin, you'll be my woman
like all the servants I have bled.
My wife of daybreak fed my rest
for hunger and the blood of flesh.
My daylight wife brought operators,
bought dominions, blade and shield.
My twilight woman fed the garden,
gave her blood for sap and juice.
You will feed my burgeoning country,
lend me empires for my budding.

MALINCHE'S CURSE
Weave a spell then frozen women.
Give me wing-sight for my wedding.

Malinche's Leap

You should remember the leap that you took from the bridge.

In night-sleep, the island city burns.
After hours of creeping passages and alleys
with the conjured, the chimeras,
I walk a boulevard full of light
past the bleak wall of an ancient hospital,
the sunken church, the merry windows:
here on taking a wrong turn you find me

– those street-children mouthing peso,
that farmer's belly with its empty sag,
the prostitute's poverty, the drug-ridden fool,
the executioner and disappeared,
these dead masses writhing in the soft earth,
the dead blood pumped into city chambers,
the lost aspirations of a history, this century.

Shut up in my life, the house burns.
Bridges collapse and fall into Lake Texcoco.
I stand at the edge of the broken place
where the bridge fell; from the other side
I call to you, this is my lost chance.
Behind you the forest, its wet palms
thrashing like fish, like hands in space.

The water-gap where the bridge fell is filled
by dead horses, bodies of both sexes, servants,
bundles, bags. People cross the breach treading on
corpses, horses, boxes. Looking among
the stacked dead, there is one for each year of my lives.
When I step down: my open palms, mouths.
And last the island burns in my night sleep.

THE CEDAR AND THE LONG-TAILED BIRD

THE WIVES' ENGLYN TO MALINCHE
Amidst raw livers rives stumped cedar,
livened knot of knitted hives;
branches sing of broaching scythes,
prizes stung by priesting wives.

MALINCHE'S QUESTION TO THE WIVES
Here the cedar of my husband,
where he roped me for his seed.
What directs me here my mothers?
What emerges from the tree?

THE WIVES' SECOND ENGLYN TO MALINCHE
A cedar grows on the high plain of men,
sunken bedrock smokes balm rain;
crafting dam of cleft domains
knows the flood of flock and skein.

MALINCHE'S RESPONSE TO THE WIVES
Now, you speak of Cortés cursing:
he locks me from the light of day.
But I keep the plume of owling,
mapping leaf-troughs for my prey.

THE WIVES' THIRD ENGLYN TO MALINCHE
Red branches where a watch-eyed bird remains;
a haven from the blade and halberd,
here tawdry tales will be heard:
daughters must not be deterred.

MALINCHE UNDERSTANDS THE WIVES
From your mouths come feathers, plumage;
your language conjures long-tailed birds.
Beaks are roosting, wresting, netting
jewelled speech, the riotous word.

MALINCHE'S SECRET

Husband now that we have woken
Let's recount nocturnal wandering.
Let me tell how dreaming took me
at my night-time husband's bidding.

Walking lone among the cedars
was a pale majestic building
and it walked from room to chamber:
Is my own Beloved here?

Is my own Amado here?
Not a soul was living in it,
but above there was a parrot
shrieking out a lone refrain:

> THE PARROT'S LAMENT
> *Turn away you wildering bride:*
> *never at this house arrive.*

But my love, I lay here dreaming
walked with ease from room to room,
garden, armoury and country,
rooms for torture, darkening chambers.

Rooms still darkening, torture chambers,
for a grasping line of women:
Fingers, eyes and ear lobes missing.
Is my own Amado here?

> THE WIVES' LAMENT
> Woeful girl in this dank sinkhole
> cenote of murderers, thieves;
> here your husband lives and loves you
> but your flesh, he'll strip and cleave.

And no sooner than I'd hidden
– lacking weary husband's bidding,
walking lone among the cedars –
than my own Beloved rose.

Then my own Amado rose
walking loved from room to room,
past the garden, ripe with cleavers:
woeful girl for lonely chambers.

THE PARROT'S LAMENT
Turn away you shadowing bride:
never at this house arrive.

Husband, know that castle walked
its soul a string of beaded ears:
lobes of bandits, lobes of women,
gilded fingers kept in safe-box.

Fingers caught in gilded locks
of that girl who love won't live in.
Out blue fingers, out green thumbs,
grim and grinning under blankets.

THE WIVES' LAMENT
Woeful girl, whose cold love lives
in country rooms of den and sinkhole:
murderers as true as plums
falling in your ripening lap.

Husband now, you fall out tumbling
out into my very love.
And I ask you, what are sinkholes?
And I see you chopped, my dear.

Is my own Amado here?
In my very lap, a sinkhole,
cenote and den of ears.
Is my true Beloved here?

THE PARROT'S LAMENT
Turn without you murdering bride:
he will not leave this house alive.

Woeful husband, know this sinkhole:
a den of women, lobed and thumbed.
Don't forget my spearing fingers
blackened, tarred and ripe as plums.

NOTES

The Curse of the Long-tailed Bird was written out of a project with the poet Julie Boden. As Birmingham Symphony Hall poet laureate, she gathered a group of women writers together to write some poems in response to the themes of Béla Bartók's short opera, *Duke Bluebeard's Castle*. (I pastiche the *Bluebeard* libretto by Béla Balázs in exchanges between La Malinche and Cortés.) In this version, there is not one door, but seven doors that Judith must open before she discovers Bluebeard's secret: his murdered wives. I reconfigure the story in relation to the figure of Dona Marina or La Malinche, who was the woman of Hernán Cortés as well as his translator. She is an extremely ambiguous figure in Mexican history. In accounts of the conquest, she differs radically. She is by turns: passive, 'My lord, the Captain wishes to know where you are from'; authoritative, 'Mexicanos, come forward!'; and challenging, 'what can the chiefs of Tenochtitlan be thinking of?' Ultimately, her legacy in the eyes of many ordinary Mexicans is one of guilt, shame and betrayal.

In my recycling of the Bluebeard story, the guilt that the protagonist confronts is not only that of Cortés and La Malinche, but it is also the guilt of the West and developed countries. I draw on *The Open Veins of Latin America* by Eduardo Galeano, which constructs an argument that there can never be stability in Latin America as long as there are resources to be exploited.

A number of real places in Mexico feature in these poems. 'Space-Time' is based on Mexcaltitlán, an island on a lagoon in the Mexican state of Nayarit. 'The Treasury' mentions Tenochtitlan, which was the ancient city of the Aztecs destroyed by the Spanish. Mexico City was built on its ruins. I refer again to Tenochtitlan in 'The Torture Chamber' and 'La Malinche' when I mention Lake Texcoco. Tenochtitlan was built on an island in the midst of this lake, which was later drained to allow the expansion of Mexico City. I mention Copper Canyon in 'The Dark', which is a magnificent landmark of the Sierra Tarahumara and I also refer to Loreto, a small settlement in these mountains.

As a writer, I am very interested in intertextuality. The epigraphs draw on the following sources:

1. **The Torture Chamber:** *The forms of public order are authorised to punish with the aid of appropriate weapons.* Injunctions like this one legitimised the brutalisation of latifundio workers in banana republics like Guatemala, Honduras, Costa Rica, Panama, Colombia, Ecuador and even Mexico to some extent.

2. **The Armoury:** *Fortune favours the daring.* These words were reportedly said by Cortés, who mortgaged everything he owned to equip his Mexican expedition.

3. **The Treasury:** *Father a merchant, son a gentleman, grandson a beggar.* A Mexican proverb.

4. **The Garden:** *Is building on sugar better than building on sand?* This was the comment of Jean-Paul Sartre on visiting Cuba in 1960. His comment applies to all of the South American countries where monocultures prevail.

5. **The Far Country:** *We had to get rid of a Communist government which had taken over.* This was Dwight D. Eisenhower's comment, years after his actions, about his interference in the politics of Central America, particularly Guatemala.

6. **The Dark:** *There are no accomplices here other than you and I. You as oppressor, I as liberator, deserve to die.* These are reportedly the last words of Tupac Amaru, a mestizo chief and descendant of the Inca emperors. He was tortured and put to death by the Spanish.

7. **The Wives:** *The sleeping woman slowly eats her midnight heart.* This was inspired by an untitled Alejandra Pizarnik poem:

> Zona de plagas donde la dormida come
> lentamente
> su corazón de medianoche.

TRANSLATIONS

Blodeuwedd (18)

Pan yr wyf i'n agos...o flaen y tân: 'When I am close to the house in the dark, I see the window is bright and when I arrive, I travel in to hurl myself on the red carpet, warm and soft in front of the fire.'
a'r defaid...am siswrn: 'and the sheep calling outside. I pick a leaf from one leg, stand, look in the cupboard for a scissors.'
ond...blodau gwlyb: '...but I still trim the wet flowers.'
Mae'n un ffordd i fyw: 'It's one way to live.'

The Secret (30)

I quote T.H. Parry William's 'Hon': *Dyma'r Wyddfa a'i chriw; dyma lymder a moelni'r tir*: 'Here is Snowdon and her crew; here is poverty and the barrenness of the land.' 'She' (35) is my version of this poem.

The Orphic Principle (33-34)

Yr un a wnaeth gwae dan f'ais, cyffyrddwch sŵn fy llef: 'The one who made the ache under my ribs, touch the sound of my cry.' *Garaf ac y gerais*: 'I love and I loved.' *Blodyn y gwynt ydw i*: 'I am the wind flower.' *Blodeuyn yr eira ydw i*: 'I am the blossom of snow.' *Ffrwyth y tarannau ydw i*: 'I am the thunder's fruit.'

GLOSSARY

bethma: what-do-you-call-it.
Blodeuwedd: literally 'flower face'; the story from the Mabinogion tells of a woman made of flowers, who later is punished by Gwydion, the magician, and turned into an owl.
brain: crows.
brân: a crow (Branwen's brother in the Mabinogion).
branwen: white crow (a princess in the Mabinogion).
bytholwyrdd: evergreen.
castell: a castle.
cilfach cefn: a backwater.
coron: a crown.
crafangau: talons.
dicllon: angry.
distawrwydd: silence.
Gororau: borders (the Marches).
gwreiddiau: roots.
gwres: warmth; **gwresog**: warm.
mamiaith: mother-tongue.
peren ac afal: pear and apple.
teithwyr: travellers.
tŵr: a tower.
ysbryd: a spirit or ghost.